CRACOW
by Night

CRACOW *by Night*

ADAM **BUJAK**　　　　MARCIN **BUJAK**

Layout and Publishing Concept:

LESZEK SOSNOWSKI

HISTORY OF CRACOW: KEY DATES

7th-8th century.	The mounds of Krakus and Wanda, the legendary founder of the city and his daughter, were built. Their existence proves the presence of developed settlements and social life within the territory of today's Cracow.
9th century	Cracow presumably functioned as a capital of the Vistulans' state.
965/966	Ibrahim ibn Yaqub, a Jewish merchant, writing about his travels, mentioned Karako (Cracow) as a populous city and an important commercial centre located in the Czech kingdom.
Ca. 990	Mieszko I annexed Cracow to his kingdom.
1000	The establishing of a new Church structure in Poland was announced during a meeting between Boleslaus the Brave and emperor Otto III. One of the new bishoprics subordinate to the Gniezno metropolitan was founded in Cracow.
1045 or 1046	The Cracow Diocese was taken over by the Tyniec Benedictine abbot, Aaron. As Bretislaus I destroyed Gniezno and Poznań, Aaron became the archbishop and acted as the supreme head of the entire Polish Church.
1079	In the conflict between king Boleslaus the Brave, called also Generous and the Bishop of Cracow, Stanislaus of Szczepanów, the latter died a martyr's death.
1138	Cracow was granted the function of the high duchy by the power of a succession statute of Boleslaus the Wrymouth within the state divided into provinces. Political and military rivalry between Piast dukes for the reign over the city started.
1184	The relics of an early Christian martyr, Florian, arrived from Rome upon the order of Bishop Gedko and were deposited in the Cathedral on Wawel Hill.
1222	Bishop Iwo Odrowąż bestowed the parish Church of the Holy Trinity upon the Order of the Dominican Friars.
1237	The Order of the Franciscan Fathers arrived from Prague.
1241	The great Tartar invasion caused significant destruction to the city.
1253	St Stanislaus was canonised in Assisi. The cult of this new saint was associated with the idea of the restitution of the Polish kingdom.
5th June 1257	In a village of Kopernia, Prince Boleslaus the Shy with his mother Grzymisława and wife Cunegunda issued Cracow's location privilege based on the Magdeburg law. Thus, a completely new regular chess-board city layout, preserved until today, was set out. A square was outlined in the very centre of the city, measuring approximately 200 x 200 m. One of the greatest and most modern urban concepts of the Europe of that time was developed, functioning until this day!
1259/1260	The second Tartar invasion ravaged the city.
1285	Leszek the Black permitted the construction of fortifications around the city.
1287/88	The third, and last, Tartar invasion.
Ca. 1298	The construction of stone defensive walls was initiated during the reign of King Wenceslaus II.
1311/1312	A revolt of German townsmen against the supremacy of Prince Ladislaus the Short was lead by the headman of the city, Albert.
20th Jan. 1320	The coronation of Ladislaus the Short was held in the Cathedral on Wawel Hill. Cracow becomes the capital of the revived state from then on.
1335	King Casimir the Great founded Kazimierz, a new town next to Cracow.
7th Sep. 1358	Casimir the Great issued a grand privilege modifying rules for city organisation.
12th May 1364	Casimir the Great founded a university in Cracow.
1366	Another town was founded in the northern outskirts of the city, Kleparz. It was called Florence after the Collegiate Church of St Florian. The tri-city was finally shaped and continued in this form until the end of the 18th century.

15th Feb. 1386	The Supreme Prince of Lithuania, Jagiello and his brothers were baptised in the Cracow Cathedral. Jagiello assumed the name Ladislaus. The Polish-Lithuanian union was established through his marriage with Hedwig of Andechs ruling Poland at that time.
26th July 1400	Ladislaus Jagiello, with the last will of his wife Hedwig (d. 1399), re-established the academy today known as Jagiellonian University.
25th Nov. 1411	Fifty one Teutonic war banners captured in the battle of Grunwald were displayed at the altar of St Stanislaus in the Wawel Cathedral.
1477-89	Veit Stoss sculpted a new retable of the main altar for the Church of St Mary, the largest piece of art of this type in late-Medieval Europe.
1498-1499	During the times of King John Albert, the Barbican, a magnificent masterpiece of cefensive architecture, was built to defend the city from the direction of Kleparz.
10th Apr. 1525	King Sigismund I received the oath of homage from the Prussian Duke Albert of Hohenzollern.
8th June 1533	Bishop Piotr Tomicki consecrated a chapel adjacent to the Cracow Cathedral, built by Bartolommeo Berrecci following the orders of Sigismund I. It was one of the most outstanding achievements of Renaissance architecture north of the Alps.
15th Oct.-29th Nov. 1587	The armies of Archduke Maximilian surrounded Cracow. The city, faithful to Sigismund III Vasa, repelled the siege.
29th Jan. 1595	A huge fire in the northern wing of the Wawel Castle destroyed a considerable part of the magnificently furnished interiors. Such Italian architects as Giovanni Trevano, and stonemasons and painters like Tommaso Dolabella rebuilt the destroyed rooms according to early Roman Baroque canons following the order of Sigismund III.
1609	Sigismund III left Cracow for Smoleńsk never to return to the capital. In 1611 he settled down in Warsaw, moving there the political centre of the Polish-Lithuanian state. Cracow continued to be the official capital of Poland down to the time of partitions.
25th Sep. -18th Oct 1655	After a fierce defence of the city commanded by Stefan Czarniecki, Cracow, outnumbered by the superior powers of the Swedish King Charles Gustav, was forced to surrender. During the defence, the city outskirts were destroyed as well as some of the buildings within the city walls. The destructive Swedish occupation began. The Swedes plundered churches, monasteries, private homes and enforced contributions on citizens.
24th Aug. 1657	The Swedish armies occupying Cracow surrendered. Although the reconstructions were carried out throughout the following decades, the city never returned to its previous grandeur.
10th Aug.-12th Oct. 1702	Cracow was conquered by Charles XII, King of Sweden. A great fire (15th-18th September) destroyed a larger part of the royal castle on Wawel Hill, along with its Renaissance and Baroque interior decorations.
14th Oct. 1703	The newly erected university Church of St Anna was officially consecrated. The church was one of the most outstanding late-Baroque buildings in Central Europe owing its uniqueness to the design of Tylman van Gameren and interior decorative sculptures by Baltasar Fontana.
1707-1708	A sweeping epidemic of typhoid fever annihilated over 7,000 human lives.
17th Jan. 1734	The last coronation in the Wawel Cathedral took place: Augustus III of the Wettin dynasty received the Polish crown.
1768-1772	Cracow participated in the events of the Bar Confederation. The confederates who seized the Wawel Castle on 2nd February 1772 gained special glory.
1772	The town of Kazimierz was captured by Austrian troops.
1776	The town of Kazimierz was reinstated into the Republic of Poland. The "Good Order Commission" initiated its restoration activities in Cracow.
1780	As a result of an extensive reform in the education system, the Cracow Academy was modernised and renamed the Principal School of the Realm.

HISTORY OF CRACOW: KEY DATES

28th Feb. 1784	The Austrian Emperor Joseph II issued a location patent for Podgórze, a town on the right bank of the Vistula River, seized by the Austrians in the first partition of Poland.
16th-29th June 1787.	The only visit of King Stanislaus Augustus Poniatowski to the city
1792-1794	Cracow continued to remain under the Russian occupation.
24th Mar. 1794	The insurrection against the Russian rule began with an oath by Tadeusz Kościuszko in the city square.
15th June 1794	Cracow surrendered to the Prussians.
1795	The Prussians seized the crown insignia from the Crown Treasury on Wawel Hill.
5th Jan. 1796	Austrian armies entered Cracow and incorporated the city as part of the Austrian empire.
1800	The town of Kazimierz was annexed to Cracow.
15th July 1809	The armies of Price Joseph Poniatowski entered the city. As a result, Cracow and Podgórze were annexed to the Duchy of Warsaw (14th October).
13th May 1813	Following Napoleon's defeat, the city was seized by the Russians for two years.
13th May 1815	Based on the decision of the partitioning powers, a miniature puppet republic (formally autonomous, yet actually subservient) was established: the Free, Independent, and Strictly Neutral City of Cracow with its Territory, commonly referred to as the Republic of Cracow.
23rd July 1817	The body of Prince Joseph Poniatowski was buried in the catacombs of the Cracow Cathedral, giving rise to a tradition to bury national heroes on Wawel Hill.
23rd June 1818	The temporal remains of Tadeusz Kościuszko were placed in a sarcophagus next to the tomb of Joseph Poniatowski.
1820-1823	A mound in honour of Tadeusz Kościuszko was built.
1846	An uprising against the Austrians broke out in Cracow on 22nd February. It was quickly suppressed and ended with annexing the Free City of Cracow as part of Austria.
1847	A railway line was opened connecting Cracow with Mysłowice.
Mar.-Apr. 1848	Anti-Austrian movements were brutally suppressed by the authorities. The city was bombarded from Wawel Hill.
1850	The Austrians began the construction of huge fortifications (now referred to as the Cracow Stronghold), which did not allow for free development of the city during the decades to come.
18th July 1850	The greatest fire in the history of the city broke out. Thousands of citizens lost their property and homes. The interior decorations and collections of the Franciscan and Dominican churches as well as those of the Bishops' Palace and the Wielopolski Family Palace were completely destroyed.
1866	Local government was restored in Cracow, allowing for the development of the city and its modernisation under the management of outstanding mayors: Józef Dietl, Mikołaj Zyblikiewicz and Julisz Leo.
1876	After transferring the great collection of art and historical artefacts from Paris, Prince Władysław Czartoryski opened the Princes Czartoryski Museum in Cracow, most famous for its Lady with an Ermine painted by Leonardo da Vinci.
1893	The construction of a new and impressive City Theatre, designed by Jan Zawiejski, was completed. Now it is called the Juliusz Słowacki Theatre.
21st Nov. 1896	The Cracow Heritage Society was founded.
4th July 1890	The remains of Adam Mickiewicz were brought from Paris and ceremoniously buried on Wawel Hill.
1st Apr. 1910	A number of neighbouring communes was annexed to Cracow, initiating the so-called Great Cracow project.
15th July 1910	The Grunwald Monument designed by Antoni Wiwulski and founded by Ignacy Jan Paderewski, was unveiled.
6th Aug. 1914	The First *Kadrowa* Staff Company of the Polish Legions led by Józef Piłsudski set out from Oleandry towards the Russian border.

1st July 1915	Podgórze was annexed to Cracow, increasing its population to 180,000 citizens.
31st Oct. 1918	Cracow liberated from the Austrian rule.
1925	By the power of the "Vixdum Poloniae" bull, the Cracow Bishopric was raised in status to a metropolis.
28th June 1927	The remains of Juliusz Słowacki, whose ashes were ceremoniously brought from France, were buried in the Wawel Cathedral catacombs.
6th Oct. 1933	In the presence of Marshal Józef Piłsudski, the last great review of the Polish cavalry was held on Błonia Commons, celebrating the 250th Anniversary of victory in the Battle of Vienna.
18th May 1935	The body of Józef Piłsudski was buried on Wawel Hill.
6th Sep. 1939	German troops entered Cracow. The city became the capital of the General Government. Hans Frank chose Wawel for his headquarters. Many public buildings were seized for the seats of the General Government offices. The removal of Poles from certain city districts and the Germanisation process was initiated.
6th Nov. 1939	German authorities entrapped 183 staff members of Cracow universities and academies during the action codenamed *Sonderaktion Krakau.*
13th-14th Mar. 1943	Germans brutally liquidated the Cracow ghetto, murdering some Jews on the spot and transporting the majority of inhabitants to concentration camps.
18th Jan. 1945	The Red Army entered the city, forcing the German troops to flee.
3rd May 1946	A spontaneous pro-independence demonstration took place to commemorate the 3rd May Constitution Day.
1950	The construction of a huge metallurgical plant, named after Vladimir Ilyich Lenin, was launched near Cracow. Earlier, the erection of the model socialistic town of Nowa Huta (New Steelworks) was started. It became a district of Cracow.
1951	Cardinal Adam Stefan Sapieha died. During the occupation he was referred to as the Steadfast Prince. His burial ceremony, conducted by Primate Stefan Wyszyński, became a large-scale national manifestation.
28th Sep. 1958	Karol Wojtyła received Episcopal consecration in the Wawel Cathedral.
18th Jan. 1964	Bishop Karol Wojtyła received the dignity of the Cracow Metropolitan.
7th May 1977	Stanisław Pyjas, a student, was murdered by the Security Services for political reasons. The circumstances of his death remain unexplained till this day.
23rd Sept. 1978	The historical Cracow centre was entered into the First UNESCO World Cultural and Natural Heritage List.
16th Oct. 1978	The Cracow Metropolitan Karol Wojtyła was elected in Rome as the successor of St Peter and took on the name of John Paul II.
6th-10th June 1979	John Paul II visited Cracow for the fist time. He celebrated High Mass on Wawel Hill, upon the relics of St Stanislaus, the Cracow bishop, to commemorate the 900th Anniversary of the bishop's martyrdom.
18th Mar. 1980	Walenty Badylak immolated himself on the Main Market Square, protesting against the code of silence surrounding the Katyń massacre.
21st Aug. 1980	A strike was organised in the rolling mill of the Lenin Steelworks.
17th May 1981	The White March, a huge silent march of Cracovians dressed in white was organised after the attempted assassination of John Paul II, becoming a mass collective prayer in the intention to save the Holy Father.
2000	In the jubilee year, Cracow performed, the honourable role as one of the official cultural capitals of Europe.
2002	John Paul II visited Cracow for the last time.
2006	Cracow visited by Pope Benedict XVI.

Prepared by Krzysztof Czyżewski

Wawel, a limestone hill facing the Vistula River, was the seat of rulers since ancient times. Krakus,
the legendary founder of Cracow, is said to have ruled here. Previous page: Cracow viewed from Podgórze.

In the year 1000, the cathedral church of the Cracow bishop
was erected close to the residence of princes and kings.

Two huge fire towers, Senatorska and Sandomierska, built in the second half of the 15th century, prove that Wawel performed the role of a stronghold for several centuries.

Towering castle walls testify to the brilliant
past of Cracow and Poland.

The cathedral clock has a biblical quotation, "Vigilate, quia nescitis diem neque horam",
i.e. Be vigilant, for you not know the day or the time..."

Tadeusz Kościuszko buried in the undergrounds of the cathedral, the national Pantheon. His monument was erected in 1921 at the entrance gate to Wawel.

A Gothic residential tower, called Danish, faces the city, protruding from the Renaissance royal castle block. It was topped with an alcove in the 16th century with a superior view of the surroundings. Close by, a bay window is set on slim pillars, referred to as Kurza Stopka (Hen's Foot).

►

"Non nobis Domine, non nobis, sed nomini Tuo da gloriam:"
Not us, our Lord, not us, but Your name be praised...

...Sigismund I the Old ordered this sentence to be inscribed on his burial chapel in the cathedral.
Bartolommeo Berrecci (1519-1533) designed this masterpiece of Renaissance architecture.

Most of the Polish kings were buried within the Wawel Cathedral. Among the monarch tombstones, under a canopy, stands out Ladislaus Jagiello's (d. 1434) sarcophagus. Jagiello was the first ruler of the Polish Kingdom united with the Great Lithuanian Principality.

Prayer on All Souls' Day in the Świętokrzyska Chapel, where Casimir Jagiellon (d. 1492) and his wife, Elżbieta Rakuszanka (d. 1505) are buried. Cardinal Franciszek Macharski celebrates the ceremony.

Year in year out, on 2nd November, a procession circles the cathedral to the low,
rhythmic sound of the Sigismund Bell.

The altar with relics of the Homeland's patron, St Stanislaus, is located in the centre of the Cracow Cathedral. At very special events liturgy is celebrated in this place nowadays, just as it was in the old times. On 13th October, 2003, Reverend Professor Stanisław Nagy, appointed cardinal by John Paul II, received Episcopal ordinations here.

On All Souls' Day, the Paschal candle and the figure of the Risen Christ are placed at the main altar along with symbols of royal power (the crown and the sceptre) and of sacerdotal dignity (the mitre and the chalice with a paten).

The royal castle courtyard, surrounded with Renaissance galleries, was once the maidan where tournaments for knights were held. Now it hosts concerts and theatre performances.

MAIN MARKET SQUARE

The present-day magnificent building of the Cloth Hall was erected in the following century, but it owes its shape to two major reconstructions. After the 1555 fire, the high attic with mascarons was built. The arcades were completed in the years 1875-1879 to the design of Tomasz Pryliński. Cabs are no longer parked at the Cloth Hall, but tourists who need elegance may be satisfied with varnished, brand new and glittering carriages.

The first Cloth Hall building was located in the centre of the city, in the market square,
as early as in the second half of the 13th century.

The café, which continues traditions of the confectionery established in 1823 by the Cortesi, Redolfi and Maurizio families, finds pride in its history.

Nightlife entertainment in the Main Market Square in summer time is mostly concentrated in the so-called street gardens, belonging to numerous restaurants and cafés.

Flowers may be bought in the market stalls even at night.

Streets and pavements were recently renewed, and street lamps were set up resembling historical patterns, thus fully justifying the common name used for the Cracow market square: the city showroom.

On the periphery of the Old Town, there are places
which encourage rest over a cup of coffee,
and maybe something more...
The romantic street garden in the pavilion of the Office
for Artistic Exhibitions is located in the area of Planty Park.

Beer from Świdnica used to be served in the basement
of the Town Hall. Nowadays, an open air café stands at
the Gothic Town Hall Tower.

Tourists from all over the world sit
at the tables close to the Polonia House.

In the 1980s, several historical performances were organised at the initiative of Piotr Skrzynecki and "Piwnica pod Baranami", such as "The Entrance of Prince Joseph Poniatowski to Cracow in the Year 1809" and the "Prussian Homage in 1525" (in the photo).

Fireworks have been illuminating important
and joyful ceremonies in the city for several centuries.

The Cloth Hall at the ceremony organised to celebrate Poland joining the European Union.
A huge flag of the united Europe was set up in May 2004 on the Town Hall Tower. (right)

A sculpture referring directly to ancient Greek culture
was donated to Cracow by its author, Igor Mitoraj.

The Church of St Adalbert was erected in the 12th century to replace the former wooden temple. Its unusual location (within the market square) is a remnant of the early-Medieval settlement system, changed as a result of setting out a new regular layout related to the great location in 1257. Middle-class town houses and magnate palaces are in the background. In the foreground: the 1898 monument of Adam Mickiewicz by Teodor Rygier.

St Mary's Square was once a church cemetery. The 16th-17th century townsfolk grave chapels survived until this day, adjacent to the temple of St Mary and the Church of St Barbara.

The fountain designed by Jan Budziłło was placed in the centre of the area in 1958. It is
topped with the figure taken after one of the statuettes ornamenting the frame of the main
scene in the Veit Stoss altar in the Church of St Mary.

Two towers of different heights in the main parish church of the Assumption of the Blessed Virgin Mary form the most characteristic feature of the Cracow panorama. The Gothic building was erected in stages in the 14th and 15th centuries.

The pr de of Cracow is its altar, made by Veit Stoss
in the years 1477-1489, the largest late-Gothic altar in Europe.

The Veit Stoss altar consist of a cabinet with figures and two pairs of
wings (moving and fixed), divided into quarters.

Scenes from the life of Christ and Mary. The central part of the altar (in the photo) depicts two episodes from Mary's life: the Dormition and the Assumption.

Collegium Novum, built in the years 1883-1887 to the design of Feliks Księżarski, is the seat of authorities of the oldest Polish university, which was established in 1364 by Casimir the Great.

The Gothic Collegium Maius received its final form at the turn of the 16th century.
The Jagiellonian University Museum is now located here.

The monument of the famous student of the Cracow Academy, Nicolaus Copernicus, sculptured by Cyprian Godebski in 1900.

Royal and episcopal coats-of-arms are displayed above the main gate to Collegium Maius.

The city arsenal built by Gabriel Słoński in the years 1565-1566, rebuilt in 1854-1861. Once it was a storehouse for cannons and other city arms; now it holds the exhibition of antiques of the Princes Czartoryski Museum.

Remains of Medieval defence walls are preserved within the premises
of the Dominican Sisters monastery in Gródek.
Even elements of the original Butcher's Gate survived here.

The only section of the former city fortifications preserved
in the form similar to the original, closing the Old Town from the north.

Stone defence walls reinforce the Pasamoników, Stolarska and Ciesielska bastions. In the centreline of Floriańska Street, a gate is located of the same name (St Florian's Gate). At the end of the 15th century, a huge fortified building was erected in front of Floriańska Gate: the Barbican. Its silhouette combines nicely with the lofty figure of King Ladislaus Jagiello, at the top of the monument in Matejko Square, erected in 1910 to commemorate the 500th Anniversary of the Battle of Grunwald.

The Papal Days dedicated to the most renowned Cracow citizen,
John Paul II, were inaugurated in October 2004 by Cardinal Franciszek Macharski.

The ceremonial completion of the diocese information process
on the heroic nature of virtues of the Servant of the Lord, John Paul II (the Wawel Cathedral).

The producers of the film on John Paul II during the grand Polish premiere
in the building of the Cracow Philharmonic Hall.

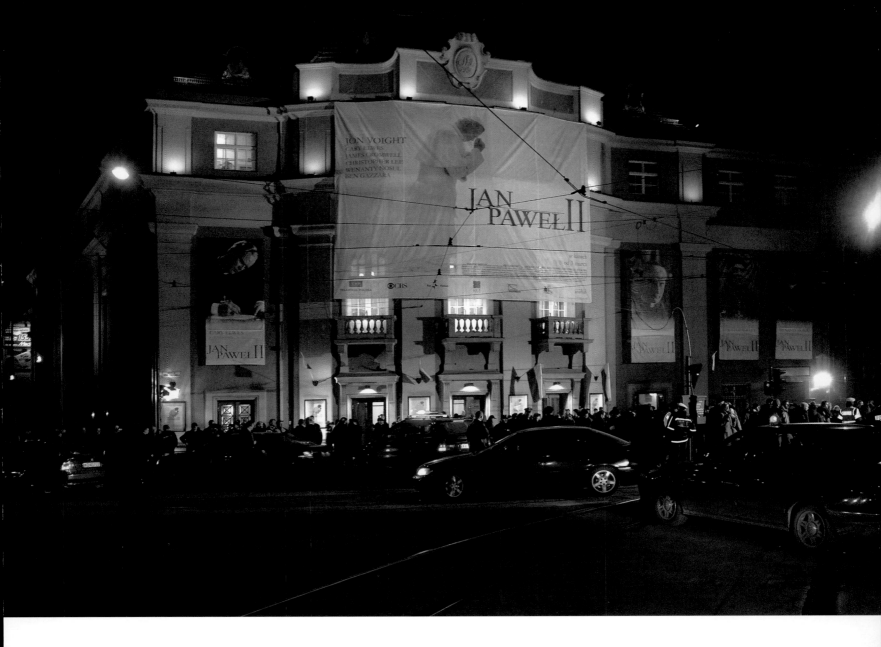

The Catholic House built in the years 1928-1931
following the initiative of Cardinal Adam Stefan
Sapieha, now housing the Philharmonic Hall, in a
special decoration prepared for the premiere of the
filmed biography of Karol Wojtyła, John Paul II.

Cracow remembers and will always remember its great shepherd, Karol Wojtyła, Metropolitan of Cracow in the years 1964-1978, who led the entire Church as John Paul II from 1978 to 2005.
Numerous monuments are simply tokens of the actual respect and love for him from millions of people all over the world. The photo shows the monument by Czesław Dźwigaj, in Rakowice.

The Rakowice Cemetery,
Monument to Victims of Communism.

Cracow artists carolling in a homely spirit. Right to left: Anna Dymna, Krzysztof Orzechowski, Andrzej Sikorowski, Chariklia Sikorowska, Barbara Lisowska Geber, Andrzej Lisowski, Ewa Bujak.

Christmas Eve at Wawel Hill.

Bitter cold is not a problem for young Cracow citizens, who come
with their parents to the Nativity Scene in the Franciscan Church.

For years, Cracow sons to St Francis have been restoring the splendid tradition of live Christmas Nativity Scenes.

Both people and animals play their roles in the biblical drama.

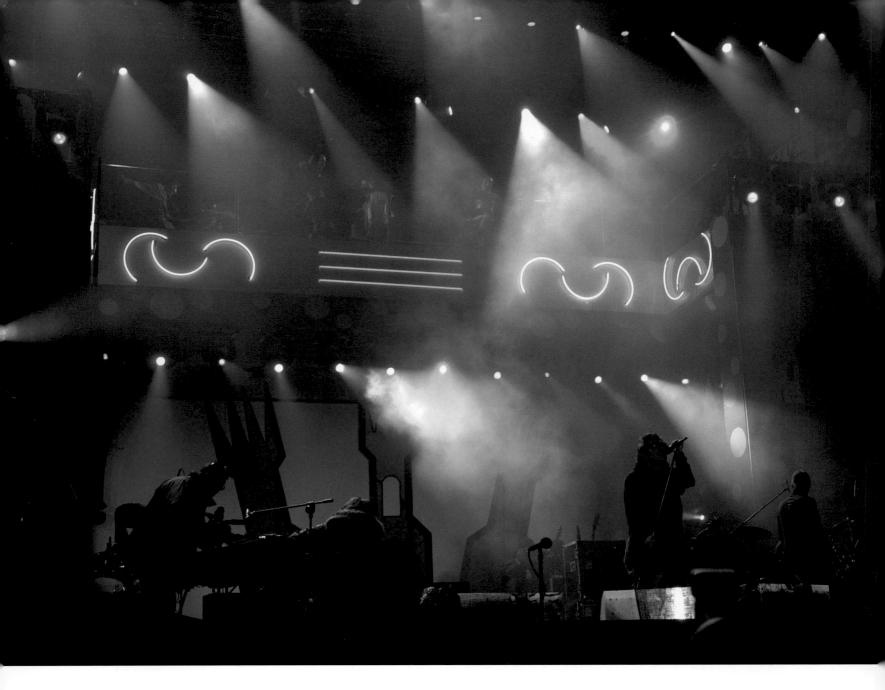

The New Year's Eve celebration
in the Main Market Square.

Welcoming the New Year in Cracow:
the largest open-air festivity in Poland.

Time for entertainment for the people of Cracow,
but also for visitors from other parts of Poland and the world.

Organisers do their best to offer
new attractions every year.

Time for reflection after the carnival: Lent in Cracow is
an especially intense experience in the Franciscan Church.

"Stabat Mater Dolorosa" (Sorrowful Mother), a profoundly moving text dedicated
to the Passion of Christ, echoes during the Passion procession in the monastery galleries.

The Chapel of Lord's Passion, famous for stations of the Way of the Cross painted by Józef Mehoffer,
is the scenery of worship services celebrated on every Friday of the Holy Week.

The Jerusalem worship services
always gathers many followers.

Members of the Archconfraternity use traditional black robes
and canes with vanitative and passion motifs.

◄
The Archconfraternity of the Holy Agony of Our Lord Jesus Christ, established
in 1595 by canon Marcin Szyszkowski, the later Bishop of Cracow, participates in the liturgy.

The Archconfraternity
of Good Death.

Religious archconfraternities were most numerous in the past. Each of them was dedicated to devotion, and many of them also performed an important charity role.

"Memento homo mori" or "Remember death, oh man." This is what brothers
sing entering the chapel at the beginning of Holy Mass.

At the turn of the 20th century, the Franciscan temple, dating back to the 13th century, received magnificent painting decorations by Stanisław Wyspiański, composed of wall paintings and stained glass windows.

Windows in the chancel are ornamented with stained glass art presenting
St Francis receiving stigmas, Blessed Salomea and the four elements.

The Franciscans and the Dominicans: since the 13th century, noble
competitors and colleagues in evangelisation. The Franciscan temple on
one side of a spacious square in the centre of the city and the Dominican
temple on the other side. Monuments were erected in All Saints' Square
to commemorate two great Cracow mayors in the period of Galician
autonomy: Józef Dietl (right) and Mikołaj Zyblikiewicz.

The Dominican Gothic temple, built progressively from the mid-13th century to the 15th century, burnt entirely in 1850.
It was rebuilt with many neo-Gothic elements, like the impressive church porch, designed by Father Marian Pavoni.

The Dominican liturgy is especially attractive to followers.
The Order of Preachers enjoys high esteem among
Cracow students and intellectuals.

Grodzka Street is a place where early-Medieval Cracow, represented by the Roman temple of St Andrew neighbours with Baroque Cracow, whose grandeur is perfectly reflected in the Jesuit Church of SS Peter and Paul.

Close to the turmoil of a big city... the Sisters of St Clara support the world with silent
and persistent prayer in the monastery of the Church of St Andrew.

The wall that restricts physical freedom,
but offers the possibility of spiritual liberation.

The monogram of the Jesus Christ's Name radiates from the centre of the facade of the Church of SS Peter and Paul. It is the emblem of the Jesuits, who exercised ministry in this church until the order was abolished in 1773.

The oldest Polish monastery of Friars Minor of the Regular Observance (called Bernardines) is located in Cracow. Cardinal Zbigniew Oleśnicki, moved by the speeches of St John Capistrano, staying in the city at that time, settled the friars in Stradom at the foot of Wawel Hill in 1453. The original Bernardine Church was destroyed during the Swedish siege of Cracow in 1655. The present, Baroque building, was erected in the years 1659-1680.

One of the chapels houses the grave of Blessed Szymon of Lipnica,
who served at the convent from 1457 to 1482.

The Collegiate Church of St Florian since 1184. The town founded here by
Casimir the Great was called Florence after the name of its patron (today known as Kleparz).

The miraculous intervention and saving of the church during the fire of Kleparz (1528) was attributed to St Florian.

The Salwator cemetery chapel was erected recently according to the design of Witold Cęckiewicz.

The sign of salvation overlooks the city of the dead and the living.

▶

◄

A rare example of wooden architecture in Cracow: the Chapel of St Margaret built in the 17th century.

The Sacrosanct Salvator Church includes parts of Roman constructions. Its present-day form dates back to the first half of the 17th century.

95

The Norbertine Sisters settled down in Zwierzyniec, near Cracow, as early as mid-12th century. The church dedicated to St Augustine and St John the Baptist is located in the centre of the monastic complex. Roman and Gothic walls are hidden under the architecture of the first half of the 17th century. Classical interior decorations of the temple chancel, unique in Cracow, deserve special attention.

The entire Norbertine building complex is of a clearly defensive nature,
which was due to the location of the monastery outside of the city walls.

Night illumination outlines the major parts of the buildings in the dark.
The towers of the Church on the Rock soar high above the arch structure of the Józef Piłsudski Bridge.

The bell tower in the Church of St Joseph in Podgórze, despite its modest architecture, creates a monumental impression protruding from the top of the limestone rock.

In 1784, the Austrian Emperor, Joseph II issued the location edict for a new town on the right bank of the Vistula River, facing Kazimierz. Podgórze remained independent up to 1915, when it voluntarily merged with Cracow, being one of its major districts ever since. The neo-Gothic parish Church of St Joseph built in the years 1905-1909 according to the design of Jan Sas-Zubrzycki, stands in the upper part of the former town's square.

The Jurassic hillocks of Krzemionki form the towering background for the Church of St Joseph. The extremely picturesque Bednarski Park, named after its founder, was established here in 1896.

The Rock (Skałka), although located in the very heart of a big metropolis, preserved its special character. Bordered with former Pauline and Augustinian gardens on one side and adjacent to Vistula promenades, it is a superior place for rest and repose.

The 1894-1895 gate, ornamented with crests of the Polish Kingdom, the Great Lithuanian Principality, St Stanislaus and the Pauline Order.

A place, sanctified with St Stanislaus' blood, was given in 1472 to the Paulines invited from Jasna Góra by Jan Długosz.

The Bishop of Cracow, Stanislaus of Szczepanów, suffered a martyr's death in the Church on the Rock in 1079.

Spiritual sons to St Paul I the Hermit systematically popularise the cult of the most significant Polish patron.

"Veraicon"
from the Rock collections.

The 1738 picture presents St Stanislaus as the intercessor pleading with God
for Cracow and Poland. The Rock settlement is visible at the bottom.

The sarcophagus of an outstanding painter, Henryk Siemiradzki (the author of the famous stage curtain in the Juliusz Słowacki Theatre), sculptured according to the design of Karol Knaus in 1904.

The final resting place for distinguished Poles was established in the years 1876-1880 in the lower Church on the Rock. The altar holds the image of Our Lady of Częstochowa, and the walls are ornamented with painted coats-of-arms of Polish lands. Sarcophagi for eminent Poles were placed at the walls and in deep niches.

The vaults of Henryk Siemiradzki (left), Karol Szymanowski
(in the background) and Józef Ignacy Kraszewski (right).

Once popular and now almost forgotten poet, Wincenty Pol, is among the people honoured with burial in the Vault of Meritorious. An outstanding mathematician, Tadeusz Banachiewicz, rests beside.

In 2004, the Literary Nobel Prize laureate, Czesław Miłosz, found eternal rest on the Rock. The poet settled down in Cracow for the last years of his long and rich life. The most well-known Cracow poet, an eminent painter and true visionary, Stanisław Wyspiański, also buried on the Rock. The figures of St Stanislaus and his assassin, prince Boleslaus the Bold, continuously appear through Wyspiański's literary and graphic work. Their dramatic conflict, which ended with tragic events on the Rock, haunted Wyspiański for years.

Stanisław Wyspiański rests in a monumental sarcophagus
designed by Jana Rzymkowski in 1912.

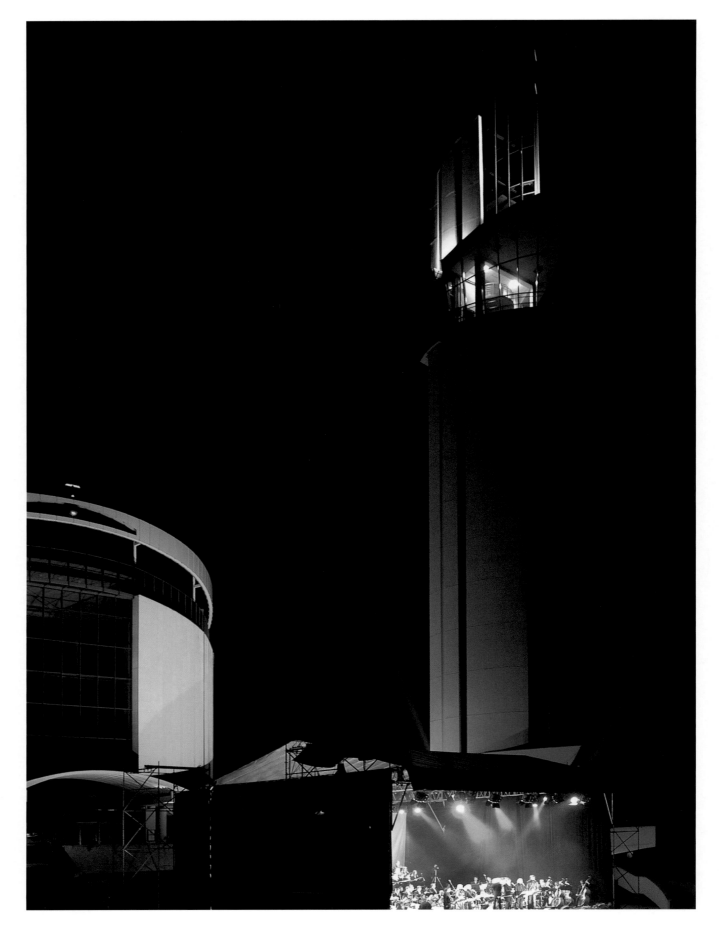

The most recent Cracow sanctuary, the Church of the Divine Mercy in Łagiewniki, founded close to the small monastery of the Sister's of the Congregation of Our Lady of Mercy, where St Faustina Kowalska lived and died.

Cardinal Karol Wojtyła was an ardent promoter of the Divine Mercy cult. When he became Pope John Paul II, he spread it throughout the Church. His successor in Cracow, Cardinal Franciszek Macharski (photo), assumed the phrase "Jesu, in Te confido" (Jesus, I trust in You) as his motto. It was he who initiated the construction of the world centre of the Divine Mercy (designed by Witold Cęckiewicz) along with the church consecrated in 2002 by John Paul II.

The hill called Sikornik was regarded as sanctified by Blessed Bronisława, who used to pray here in solitude. Close to her hermitage, the mound commemorating Tadeusz Kościuszko was constructed in the years 1820-1823.

When the Austrians surrounded the Kościuszko Mound with fortifications in the mid-19th century, Feliks Księżarski designed a neo-Gothic chapel dedicated to Blessed Bronisława.
The environs of Cracow are culturally diversified. Bielany with the Camaldolite hermitage (far right) and Tyniec with the Benedictine monastery have been particularly famous for a long time. The Vistula River can be seen at the bottom of the photo.

The Camaldolite Order, due to its hermitage nature, established
its locations in secluded areas, usually in superbly beautiful surroundings.

The Camaldolite hermitage in Bielany near Cracow. The magnificent church was erected in the first half of the 17th century, owing its existence to the generosity of Mikołaj Wolski, the grand royal marshal.

The entire Benedictine monastic community
in Tyniec bids farewell to their fellow brother.

Tyniec: the procession of monks leaves the conventual Benedictine church to assist
the deceased to the nearby cemetery, founded in the Middle Ages next to the parish
Church of St Andrew, no longer in existence.

"Requiem aeternam dona ei Domine."
Rest eternal grant to them, Lord! The Tyniec cemetery.

The Kościuszko
Mount

Cracow is located on the edge of the limestone hill range of the Cracow and Częstochowa Jura. The rocky landscape of Twardowski Rocks became the natural background for the outdoor performance organised by the Cracow Opera: "Halka" by Stanisław Moniuszko.

Limestone rock was excavated for hundreds of years, leaving deep exploitation pits. Some of them formed extremely deep and very clean water reservoirs (Zakrzówek).

"Halka" by Stanisław Moniuszko, performed in this extraordinary surrounding,
attracted a crowd of spectators.

The Court Dance Festival has already become a regular annual cultural event in Cracow. A pageant of men and women dressed in various historical clothes captures the attention of the city inhabitants and visitors.

Polish and other dances from old times are presented on
the stage set up in the Main Market Square.

Recently, a court dance group received city patronage
and adopted the name of "Cracovia Danza" Court Ballet.

The elegance of uniforms and the charming lightness and gentleness of dresses
from the period of the Duchy of Warsaw is equally attractive nowadays.

Even antic dances
are performed.

Cracow owes Romana Agnel the opportunity
to view traditional Oriental dances.

Ballet of Modern Forms of the AGH University of Science and Technology
in Cracow was established in 1969.

The ensemble takes advantage of both traditional and modern music in its performances, and it does not shun from jazz, either. It gave numerous performances internationally, and takes pride in its many significant awards and prizes.

THEATRE

In the years 1890-1893, the building of the City Theatre was erected in the place of the Medieval Holy Spirit hospital, worthy of Cracow, an important centre of Polish theatre life in the period of annexations. Initially dedicated to Aleksander Fredro, it received the name of Juliusz Słowacki in 1909. Its stage witnessed, among other events, the world premiere of "The Wedding" by Stanisław Wyspiański (1901).

The facade of the building designed by Jan Zawiejski displays a series of sculptures, including personifications of Poetry, Drama and Comedy, along with Music, Opera and Operetta.

The Helena Modrzejewska Stary Theatre is one of the most important
contemporary stages in Poland. Krzysztof Globisz, a prominent actor, in the foreground.

Awarding the title of the national theatre for the Stary Theatre proves its significance.
Andrzej Wajda in rehearsal with Krzysztof Globisz.

Andrzej Wajda is one of the most notable
stage managers of the Stary Theatre.

The reputation of the annual Jewish Culture Festival in Cracow Kazimierz is immense. It concludes with a grand concert set in the heart of the former Jewish town, in Szeroka Street, close to the Medieval Old Synagogue.

Few followers of Judaism gather for prayer in the 16th-century synagogue named after its founder, Remu.

The famous theologian, Isserles Remu, rests in the nearby cemetery. More and more pilgrims from all over the world arrive to visit his grave.
Synagogues in Kazimierz awaken to life more often for concerts than worship services these days. The interior of the Tempel Synagogue (right) is a perfect setting for synagogue cantors and klezmer bands from around the world.

The Jewish Culture Festival. The progressive Jews synagogue, called Tempel, built in the years 1860-1862 and expanded at the end of the 19th century, luckily survived the Second World War.

Kazimierz cafés often have their interior design reminiscent of pre-war Jewish restaurants and shops, many of which existed in this district before the Second World War.

Kazimierz summer gardens attract
the youth and artists most of all.

building itself) was established
tradition from the grand feast

held by Mikołaj Wierzynek in 1364 for kings and princes,
who came to Cracow invited by Casimir the Great.

One of the rooms is decorated with beautiful paintings from the year 1800, representing the Pompeian style, favoured in the Classicist period, which derived from the fascination with decorations found in Pompeii.

As with every respectable restaurant of high aspirations,
there is the hall of knights with armour components hanging on the walls.

The interior offers an exhibition of many details of
Mediaeval architectural design, like 14th-century
brickwork wall recesses, closed with ogives supported
on a sculptured stone jester's mask.

Elements of modern,
neo-style items combine well with them.

The Portrait Room.
The restaurant awaiting its guests.

The main hall in the "Hawełka" restaurant is covered with a coffer ceiling displaying a frieze painted by Włodzimierz Tetmajer in 1920, illustrating the poem by Adam Mickiewicz, "Pani Twardowska."

Later it was taken over by the family of Macharscy, who opened a luxury restaurant in the Spiski Palace in the Main Market Square.

◄

The restaurant owes its existence to Antoni Hawełka, who established the so-called small breakfast trading in the colonial shop at the end of the 19th century.

The most famed of all Cracow cafés is "Jama Michalika" at 45 Floriańska Street. It was established in 1895 by Jan Michalik, and Young Poland artists quickly made it their favourite den, jama in Polish.

Jama Michalika was originally named
the "Lviv Confectionery."

The current, playful name was given by artists and writers gathering in the café, who formed the Cracow bohemia. In 1910, the room with the stage was built, dedicated for performances of the famous "Green Balloon" café.

"The Green Balloon" performed in the years 1905-1912,
shocking the often conservative Cracow audience.

The interior of the café was designed by Franciszek Mączyński,
its Art Nouveau furniture by Karol Frycz, and stained glass pieces by Henryk Uziembło.

The charming backstreet of
Collegium Maius in Św. Anny Street.

One of the oldest and most beautiful streets in Europe, called Kanonicza
for its palaces occupied by members of the cathedral chapter.

▶

Organisers of the traditional Wianki Festival (Floating of the Wreaths) on the Vistula River always have the dream scenery guaranteed: Wawel with its historical buildings.

The Wianki ceremony is related to the pagan rituals performed on equinox,
partially surviving in its christianised form as the St John's Night customs.

Performances usually include motifs deriving
from Cracow legends, like that of the Wawel dragon.

The content of outdoor performances
is usually of secondary nature...

...light effects and loud music
is important.

Obviously, any entertainment of this kind must end with a wonderful and long fireworks display.
Next page: Cracow is very romantic in its every nook and corner, and Planty Park proves it best!

Photographs on pages:
10-23, 32-35, 37, 40, 43-46, 48-50, 54-57, 60-62, 64-83, 86, 87, 89, 90, 92-95, 98, 100-133, 135-141, 149-155, 158, 159
Adam Bujak

Photographs on pages:
8, 24-31, 36, 38, 39, 41, 42, 47, 51-53, 58, 59, 84, 85, 88, 91, 96, 97, 99, 134, 142-148, 156-157, 160-167
Marcin Bujak

Captions
Adam Bujak, Krzysztof Czyżewski

Editing Cooperation
Jolanta Sosnowska

German Translation
Adam Sosnowski
Language Consultants
Jolanta Lenard
Otto Riegler

English Translation
LINGUA EXPERT
Aneta Ptak
Mariusz Włoczysiak
Language Consultant
Alexander Ptak

Polish Proofreading
Bogdana Kłeczkowa

Organisational Cooperation
Medienbörse

Printed in Slovakia

Biały Kruk Sp. z o.o.
ul. Szwedzka 38
PL 30-324 Kraków
tel./fax: (+48) 012 260 32 40,
012 260 32 90, 012 260 34 50
e-mail: biuro@bialykruk.pl
www.bialykruk.pl

First edition
Cracow 2006

ISBN 83-60292-21-3